★ADVENTURE CALLS★

RV LOGBOOK

"**Travel** makes one modest.
You see what a tiny place
you occupy in the **World**."
–Gustave Flaubert

RV LOG

DATE: ☀️ ⛅ ☁️ 🌧️ ⛈️ ❄️ 🌬️ ☐Hot ☐Cold ☐Mild

Traveled from _____ to _____

Route Taken: _____

Start Mileage: _____ End Mileage: _____ Total Miles Traveled: _____

Sites Along The Way:

CAMPGROUND ☆☆☆☆☆

Campground Name: _____

Address: _____

Phone: _____ GPS: _____

Site #: _____ Ideal Site # (for next time): _____

Cost: _____ ☐ day ☐ week ☐ month

Memberships: _____

Altitude: _____ ☐ First Visit ☐ Return Visit

DRIVEWAY LENGTH:

☐easy access ☐back-in ☐antenna reception
☐loop ☐pull-through ☐satellite tv
☐paved ☐restrooms ☐cable tv
☐unpaved-graded ☐pet friendly ☐wifi:
☐picnic table ☐shade-partial/full   ☐free ☐$_____
☐fire ring ☐full sun
☐water ☐laundry   cell phone carrier:
☐sewer ☐store/visitor center
☐electricity ☐pool/hot tub   phone reception
☐15 amp ☐hiking trails ☆☆☆☆☆
☐30 amp ☐fishing   water pressure
☐50 amp ☐firewood ☆☆☆☆☆

NOTES FOR NEXT TIME

(fees, check in/out times, discounts, directions, loud/quiet, etc)

NOTES

(Campground Pros/Cons, Traveling Companions, People Met, Places Visited, Things to Do, Restaurants, Journaling):

RV LOG

DATE: ☀ ⛅ ☁ 🌧 ⛈ ❄ 🌫 ☐Hot ☐Cold ☐Mild

Traveled from _____ to _____

Route Taken: _____

Start Mileage: _____ End Mileage: _____ Total Miles Traveled: _____

Sites Along The Way: _____

CAMPGROUND ☆☆☆☆☆

Campground Name: _____

Address: _____

Phone: _____ GPS: _____

Site #: _____ Ideal Site # (for next time): _____

Cost: _____ ☐ day ☐ week ☐ month

Memberships: _____

Altitude: _____ ☐ First Visit ☐ Return Visit

DRIVEWAY LENGTH:

☐easy access ☐back-in ☐antenna reception
☐loop ☐pull-through ☐satellite tv
☐paved ☐restrooms ☐cable tv
☐unpaved-graded ☐pet friendly ☐wifi:
☐picnic table ☐shade-partial/full   ☐free ☐$____
☐fire ring ☐full sun
☐water ☐laundry   cell phone carrier:
☐sewer ☐store/visitor center _____
☐electricity ☐pool/hot tub   phone reception
☐15 amp ☐hiking trails ☆☆☆☆☆
☐30 amp ☐fishing   water pressure
☐50 amp ☐firewood ☆☆☆☆☆

NOTES FOR NEXT TIME

(fees, check in/out times, discounts, directions, loud/quiet, etc)

NOTES

(Campground Pros/Cons, Traveling Companions, People Met, Places Visited,
Things to Do, Restaurants, Journaling):

RV LOG

DATE: ☀ ⛅ ☁ 🌧 ⛈ ❄ 🌫 ☐Hot ☐Cold ☐Mild

Traveled from _____ to _____

Route Taken: _____

Start Mileage: _____ End Mileage: _____ Total Miles Traveled: _____

Sites Along The Way:

CAMPGROUND ☆☆☆☆☆

Campground Name: _____

Address: _____

Phone: _____ GPS: _____

Site #: _____ Ideal Site # (for next time): _____

Cost: _____ ☐ day ☐ week ☐ month

Memberships: _____

Altitude: _____ ☐ First Visit ☐ Return Visit

DRIVEWAY LENGTH:

☐easy access ☐back-in ☐antenna reception
☐loop ☐pull-through ☐satellite tv
☐paved ☐restrooms ☐cable tv
☐unpaved-graded ☐pet friendly ☐wifi:
☐picnic table ☐shade-partial/full ☐free ☐$_____
☐fire ring ☐full sun cell phone carrier:
☐water ☐laundry
☐sewer ☐store/visitor center _____
☐electricity ☐pool/hot tub phone reception
☐15 amp ☐hiking trails ☆☆☆☆☆
☐30 amp ☐fishing water pressure
☐50 amp ☐firewood ☆☆☆☆☆

NOTES FOR NEXT TIME

(fees, check in/out times, discounts, directions, loud/quiet, etc)

NOTES

(Campground Pros/Cons, Traveling Companions, People Met, Places Visited,
Things to Do, Restaurants, Journaling):

RV LOG

DATE: ☀ ⛅ ☁ ☁ ☂ 🌧 ❄ 🌫 ☐Hot ☐Cold ☐Mild

Traveled from _____ to _____

Route Taken: _____

Start Mileage: _____ End Mileage: _____ Total Miles Traveled: _____

Sites Along The Way: _____

CAMPGROUND ☆☆☆☆☆

Campground Name: _____

Address: _____

Phone: _____ GPS: _____

Site #: _____ Ideal Site # (for next time): _____

Cost: _____ ☐ day ☐ week ☐ month

Memberships: _____

Altitude: _____ ☐ First Visit ☐ Return Visit

DRIVEWAY LENGTH:

☐ easy access
☐ loop
☐ paved
☐ unpaved-graded
☐ picnic table
☐ fire ring
☐ water
☐ sewer
☐ electricity
☐ 15 amp
☐ 30 amp
☐ 50 amp

☐ back-in
☐ pull-through
☐ restrooms
☐ pet friendly
☐ shade-partial/full
☐ full sun
☐ laundry
☐ store/visitor center
☐ pool/hot tub
☐ hiking trails
☐ fishing
☐ firewood

☐ antenna reception
☐ satellite tv
☐ cable tv
☐ wifi:
  ☐ free ☐$_____

cell phone carrier:

_____

phone reception
☆☆☆☆☆
water pressure
☆☆☆☆☆

NOTES FOR NEXT TIME

(fees, check in/out times, discounts, directions, loud/quiet, etc)

NOTES

(Campground Pros/Cons, Traveling Companions, People Met, Places Visited,
Things to Do, Restaurants, Journaling):

DATE: ☀ ⛅ ☁ ☂ ⛈ ❄ 🌫 ☐Hot ☐Cold ☐Mild

Traveled from _____ to _____

Route Taken: _____

Start Mileage: _____ End Mileage: _____ Total Miles Traveled: _____

Sites Along The Way: _____

CAMPGROUND ☆☆☆☆☆

Campground Name: _____

Address: _____

Phone: _____ GPS: _____

Site #: _____ Ideal Site # (for next time): _____

Cost: _____ ☐ day ☐ week ☐ month

Memberships: _____

Altitude: _____ ☐ First Visit ☐ Return Visit

DRIVEWAY LENGTH:

☐easy access	☐back-in	☐antenna reception
☐loop	☐pull-through	☐satellite tv
☐paved	☐restrooms	☐cable tv
☐unpaved-graded	☐pet friendly	☐wifi:
☐picnic table	☐shade-partial/full	☐free ☐$____
☐fire ring	☐full sun	**cell phone carrier:**
☐water	☐laundry	
☐sewer	☐store/visitor center	_____
☐electricity	☐pool/hot tub	**phone reception**
☐15 amp	☐hiking trails	☆☆☆☆☆
☐30 amp	☐fishing	**water pressure**
☐50 amp	☐firewood	☆☆☆☆☆

NOTES FOR NEXT TIME

(fees, check in/out times, discounts, directions, loud/quiet, etc)

NOTES

(Campground Pros/Cons, Traveling Companions, People Met, Places Visited,
Things to Do, Restaurants, Journaling):

RV LOG

DATE: ☀ 🌤 ☁ 🌦 ⛈ ❄ 🌫 ☐Hot ☐Cold ☐Mild

Traveled from _____ to _____

Route Taken: _____

Start Mileage: _____ End Mileage: _____ Total Miles Traveled: _____

Sites Along The Way:

CAMPGROUND ☆☆☆☆☆

Campground Name:

Address:

Phone: _____ GPS: _____

Site #: _____ Ideal Site # (for next time): _____

Cost: _____ ☐ day ☐ week ☐ month

Memberships:

Altitude: _____ ☐ First Visit ☐ Return Visit

DRIVEWAY LENGTH:

☐ easy access   ☐ back-in   ☐ antenna reception
☐ loop   ☐ pull-through   ☐ satellite tv
☐ paved   ☐ restrooms   ☐ cable tv
☐ unpaved-graded   ☐ pet friendly   ☐ wifi:
☐ picnic table   ☐ shade-partial/full   ☐ free ☐ $_____
☐ fire ring   ☐ full sun   **cell phone carrier:**
☐ water   ☐ laundry
☐ sewer   ☐ store/visitor center _____
☐ electricity   ☐ pool/hot tub   **phone reception**
☐ 15 amp   ☐ hiking trails   ☆☆☆☆☆
☐ 30 amp   ☐ fishing   **water pressure**
☐ 50 amp   ☐ firewood   ☆☆☆☆☆

NOTES FOR NEXT TIME

(fees, check in/out times, discounts, directions, loud/quiet, etc)

NOTES

(Campground Pros/Cons, Traveling Companions, People Met, Places Visited,
Things to Do, Restaurants, Journaling):

RV ⛰ LOG

| **DATE:** | ☀ ⛅ ☁ 🌧 ⛈ ❄ 🌫 ☐Hot ☐Cold ☐Mild |

Traveled from ＿＿＿＿＿＿＿＿ to ＿＿＿＿＿＿＿＿

Route Taken: ＿＿＿＿＿＿＿＿＿＿＿＿＿＿

Start Mileage: ＿＿＿ End Mileage: ＿＿＿ Total Miles Traveled: ＿＿＿

Sites Along The Way: ＿＿＿＿＿＿＿＿＿

CAMPGROUND ☆☆☆☆☆

Campground Name: ＿＿＿＿＿＿＿＿

Address: ＿＿＿＿＿＿＿＿＿＿＿＿

Phone: ＿＿＿＿＿ GPS: ＿＿＿＿＿＿＿

Site #: ＿＿＿＿ Ideal Site # (for next time): ＿＿＿＿

Cost: ＿＿＿＿ ☐ day ☐ week ☐ month

Memberships: ＿＿＿＿＿＿＿＿＿＿＿

Altitude: ＿＿＿＿＿＿＿ ☐ First Visit ☐ Return Visit

DRIVEWAY LENGTH:

☐easy access ☐back-in ☐antenna reception
☐loop ☐pull-through ☐satellite tv
☐paved ☐restrooms ☐cable tv
☐unpaved-graded ☐pet friendly ☐wifi:
☐picnic table ☐shade-partial/full ☐free ☐$＿＿
☐fire ring ☐full sun cell phone carrier:
☐water ☐laundry
☐sewer ☐store/visitor center ＿＿＿＿＿＿
☐electricity ☐pool/hot tub phone reception
☐15 amp ☐hiking trails ☆☆☆☆☆
☐30 amp ☐fishing water pressure
☐50 amp ☐firewood ☆☆☆☆☆

NOTES FOR NEXT TIME

(fees, check in/out times, discounts, directions, loud/quiet, etc)

NOTES

(Campground Pros/Cons, Traveling Companions, People Met, Places Visited,
Things to Do, Restaurants, Journaling):

RV LOG

DATE: ☀ ⛅ ☁ 🌧 ⛈ ❄ 🌬 ☐ Hot ☐ Cold ☐ Mild

Traveled from _____ to _____

Route Taken: _____

Start Mileage: _____ End Mileage: _____ Total Miles Traveled: _____

Sites Along The Way: _____

CAMPGROUND ☆☆☆☆☆

Campground Name: _____

Address: _____

Phone: _____ GPS: _____

Site #: _____ Ideal Site # (for next time): _____

Cost: _____ ☐ day ☐ week ☐ month

Memberships: _____

Altitude: _____ ☐ First Visit ☐ Return Visit

DRIVEWAY LENGTH:

☐ easy access
☐ loop
☐ paved
☐ unpaved-graded
☐ picnic table
☐ fire ring
☐ water
☐ sewer
☐ electricity
☐ 15 amp
☐ 30 amp
☐ 50 amp

☐ back-in
☐ pull-through
☐ restrooms
☐ pet friendly
☐ shade-partial/full
☐ full sun
☐ laundry
☐ store/visitor center
☐ pool/hot tub
☐ hiking trails
☐ fishing
☐ firewood

☐ antenna reception
☐ satellite tv
☐ cable tv
☐ wifi:
　☐ free ☐ $_____

cell phone carrier:
_____

phone reception
☆☆☆☆☆

water pressure
☆☆☆☆☆

NOTES FOR NEXT TIME

(fees, check in/out times, discounts, directions, loud/quiet, etc)

NOTES

(Campground Pros/Cons, Traveling Companions, People Met, Places Visited,
Things to Do, Restaurants, Journaling):

RV LOG

DATE: ☀ ⛅ ☁ 🌧 ⛈ ❄ 🌫 ☐Hot ☐Cold ☐Mild

Traveled from _____ to _____

Route Taken: _____

Start Mileage: _____ End Mileage: _____ Total Miles Traveled: _____

Sites Along The Way:

CAMPGROUND ☆ ☆ ☆ ☆ ☆

Campground Name: _____

Address: _____

Phone: _____ GPS: _____

Site #: _____ Ideal Site # (for next time): _____

Cost: _____ ☐ day ☐ week ☐ month

Memberships: _____

Altitude: _____ ☐ First Visit ☐ Return Visit

DRIVEWAY LENGTH:

☐ easy access ☐ back-in ☐ antenna reception
☐ loop ☐ pull-through ☐ satellite tv
☐ paved ☐ restrooms ☐ cable tv
☐ unpaved-graded ☐ pet friendly ☐ wifi:
☐ picnic table ☐ shade-partial/full ☐ free ☐ $_____
☐ fire ring ☐ full sun
☐ water ☐ laundry cell phone carrier:
☐ sewer ☐ store/visitor center _____
☐ electricity ☐ pool/hot tub phone reception
☐ 15 amp ☐ hiking trails ☆ ☆ ☆ ☆ ☆
☐ 30 amp ☐ fishing water pressure
☐ 50 amp ☐ firewood ☆ ☆ ☆ ☆ ☆

NOTES FOR NEXT TIME

(fees, check in/out times, discounts, directions, loud/quiet, etc)

NOTES

(Campground Pros/Cons, Traveling Companions, People Met, Places Visited, Things to Do, Restaurants, Journaling):

RV LOG

DATE: ☀ ⛅ ☁ 🌧 🌦 ❄ 🌬 ☐Hot ☐Cold ☐Mild

Traveled from _____ to _____

Route Taken: _____

Start Mileage: _____ End Mileage: _____ Total Miles Traveled: _____

Sites Along The Way:

CAMPGROUND ☆☆☆☆☆

Campground Name: _____

Address: _____

Phone: _____ GPS: _____

Site #: _____ Ideal Site # (for next time): _____

Cost: _____ ☐ day ☐ week ☐ month

Memberships: _____

Altitude: _____ ☐ First Visit   ☐ Return Visit

DRIVEWAY LENGTH:

☐ easy access	☐ back-in	☐ antenna reception
☐ loop	☐ pull-through	☐ satellite tv
☐ paved	☐ restrooms	☐ cable tv
☐ unpaved-graded	☐ pet friendly	☐ wifi:
☐ picnic table	☐ shade-partial/full	☐ free ☐ $____
☐ fire ring	☐ full sun	**cell phone carrier:**
☐ water	☐ laundry	
☐ sewer	☐ store/visitor center	_____
☐ electricity	☐ pool/hot tub	**phone reception**
☐ 15 amp	☐ hiking trails	☆☆☆☆☆
☐ 30 amp	☐ fishing	**water pressure**
☐ 50 amp	☐ firewood	☆☆☆☆☆

NOTES FOR NEXT TIME

(fees, check in/out times, discounts, directions, loud/quiet, etc)

NOTES

(Campground Pros/Cons, Traveling Companions, People Met, Places Visited,
Things to Do, Restaurants, Journaling):

RV ☀️ ⛅ ☁️ 🌧️ ⛈️ ❄️ 🌬️ LOG

DATE: ☐Hot ☐Cold ☐Mild

Traveled from _____ to _____

Route Taken: _____

Start Mileage: _____ End Mileage: _____ Total Miles Traveled: _____

Sites Along The Way: _____

CAMPGROUND ☆ ☆ ☆ ☆ ☆

Campground Name: _____

Address: _____

Phone: _____ GPS: _____

Site #: _____ Ideal Site # (for next time): _____

Cost: _____ ☐ day ☐ week ☐ month

Memberships: _____

Altitude: _____ ☐ First Visit ☐ Return Visit

DRIVEWAY LENGTH:

☐easy access ☐back-in ☐antenna reception
☐loop ☐pull-through ☐satellite tv
☐paved ☐restrooms ☐cable tv
☐unpaved-graded ☐pet friendly ☐wifi:
☐picnic table ☐shade-partial/full   ☐free ☐$_____
☐fire ring ☐full sun   cell phone carrier:
☐water ☐laundry
☐sewer ☐store/visitor center _____
☐electricity ☐pool/hot tub   phone reception
☐15 amp ☐hiking trails   ☆ ☆ ☆ ☆ ☆
☐30 amp ☐fishing   water pressure
☐50 amp ☐firewood   ☆ ☆ ☆ ☆ ☆

NOTES FOR NEXT TIME

(fees, check in/out times, discounts, directions, loud/quiet, etc)

NOTES

(Campground Pros/Cons, Traveling Companions, People Met, Places Visited, Things to Do, Restaurants, Journaling):

RV LOG

DATE: ☀ ⛅ ☁ 🌧 ⛈ ❄ 🌫 ☐Hot ☐Cold ☐Mild

Traveled from _____ to _____

Route Taken: _____

Start Mileage: _____ End Mileage: _____ Total Miles Traveled: _____

Sites Along The Way:

CAMPGROUND ☆☆☆☆☆

Campground Name: _____

Address: _____

Phone: _____ GPS: _____

Site #: _____ Ideal Site # (for next time): _____

Cost: _____ ☐ day ☐ week ☐ month

Memberships: _____

Altitude: _____ ☐ First Visit ☐ Return Visit

DRIVEWAY LENGTH:

☐easy access ☐back-in ☐antenna reception
☐loop ☐pull-through ☐satellite tv
☐paved ☐restrooms ☐cable tv
☐unpaved-graded ☐pet friendly ☐wifi:
☐picnic table ☐shade-partial/full   ☐free ☐$_____
☐fire ring ☐full sun   cell phone carrier:
☐water ☐laundry
☐sewer ☐store/visitor center _____
☐electricity ☐pool/hot tub phone reception
☐15 amp ☐hiking trails ☆☆☆☆☆
☐30 amp ☐fishing water pressure
☐50 amp ☐firewood ☆☆☆☆☆

NOTES FOR NEXT TIME

(fees, check in/out times, discounts, directions, loud/quiet, etc)

NOTES

(Campground Pros/Cons, Traveling Companions, People Met, Places Visited, Things to Do, Restaurants, Journaling):

RV LOG

DATE: ☀ ⛅ ☁ 🌧 ⛈ ❄ 🌬 ☐Hot ☐Cold ☐Mild

Traveled from _____ to _____

Route Taken: _____

Start Mileage: _____ End Mileage: _____ Total Miles Traveled: _____

Sites Along The Way:

CAMPGROUND ☆☆☆☆☆

Campground Name: _____

Address: _____

Phone: _____ GPS: _____

Site #: _____ Ideal Site # (for next time): _____

Cost: _____ ☐ day ☐ week ☐ month

Memberships: _____

Altitude: _____ ☐ First Visit ☐ Return Visit

DRIVEWAY LENGTH:

☐easy access   ☐back-in   ☐antenna reception
☐loop   ☐pull-through ☐satellite tv
☐paved   ☐restrooms   ☐cable tv
☐unpaved-graded ☐pet friendly ☐wifi:
☐picnic table   ☐shade-partial/full   ☐free ☐$____
☐fire ring   ☐full sun   cell phone carrier:
☐water   ☐laundry
☐sewer   ☐store/visitor center _____
☐electricity   ☐pool/hot tub   phone reception
☐15 amp   ☐hiking trails   ☆☆☆☆☆
☐30 amp   ☐fishing   water pressure
☐50 amp   ☐firewood   ☆☆☆☆☆

NOTES FOR NEXT TIME

(fees, check in/out times, discounts, directions, loud/quiet, etc)

NOTES

(Campground Pros/Cons, Traveling Companions, People Met, Places Visited, Things to Do, Restaurants, Journaling):

RV LOG

DATE: ☀ ⛅ ☁ 🌧 ⛈ ❄ 🌬 ☐Hot ☐Cold ☐Mild

Traveled from _____ to _____

Route Taken: _____

Start Mileage: _____ End Mileage: _____ Total Miles Traveled: _____

Sites Along The Way:

CAMPGROUND ☆☆☆☆☆

Campground Name: _____

Address: _____

Phone: _____ GPS: _____

Site #: _____ Ideal Site # (for next time): _____

Cost: _____ ☐ day ☐ week ☐ month

Memberships: _____

Altitude: _____ ☐ First Visit ☐ Return Visit

DRIVEWAY LENGTH:

☐easy access	☐back-in	☐antenna reception
☐loop	☐pull-through	☐satellite tv
☐paved	☐restrooms	☐cable tv
☐unpaved-graded	☐pet friendly	☐wifi:
☐picnic table	☐shade-partial/full	☐free ☐$____
☐fire ring	☐full sun	**cell phone carrier:**
☐water	☐laundry	
☐sewer	☐store/visitor center	_____
☐electricity	☐pool/hot tub	**phone reception**
☐15 amp	☐hiking trails	☆☆☆☆☆
☐30 amp	☐fishing	**water pressure**
☐50 amp	☐firewood	☆☆☆☆☆

NOTES FOR NEXT TIME

(fees, check in/out times, discounts, directions, loud/quiet, etc)

NOTES

(Campground Pros/Cons, Traveling Companions, People Met, Places Visited,
Things to Do, Restaurants, Journaling):

RV LOG

DATE: ☀ ⛅ ☁ 🌧 ⛈ ❄ 🌬 ☐Hot ☐Cold ☐Mild

Traveled from _____ to _____

Route Taken: _____

Start Mileage: _____ End Mileage: _____ Total Miles Traveled: _____

Sites Along The Way:

CAMPGROUND ☆☆☆☆☆

Campground Name: _____

Address: _____

Phone: _____ GPS: _____

Site #: _____ Ideal Site # (for next time): _____

Cost: _____ ☐ day ☐ week ☐ month

Memberships: _____

Altitude: _____ ☐ First Visit ☐ Return Visit

DRIVEWAY LENGTH:

☐easy access ☐back-in ☐antenna reception
☐loop ☐pull-through ☐satellite tv
☐paved ☐restrooms ☐cable tv
☐unpaved-graded ☐pet friendly ☐wifi:
☐picnic table ☐shade-partial/full   ☐free ☐$____
☐fire ring ☐full sun   cell phone carrier:
☐water ☐laundry
☐sewer ☐store/visitor center _____
☐electricity ☐pool/hot tub   phone reception
☐15 amp ☐hiking trails   ☆☆☆☆☆
☐30 amp ☐fishing   water pressure
☐50 amp ☐firewood   ☆☆☆☆☆

NOTES FOR NEXT TIME

(fees, check in/out times, discounts, directions, loud/quiet, etc)

NOTES

(Campground Pros/Cons, Traveling Companions, People Met, Places Visited, Things to Do, Restaurants, Journaling):

RV LOG

DATE: ☼ ⛅ ☁ 🌧 ⛈ ❄ 🌬 ☐Hot ☐Cold ☐Mild

Traveled from _____ to _____

Route Taken: _____

Start Mileage: _____ End Mileage: _____ Total Miles Traveled: _____

Sites Along The Way: _____

CAMPGROUND ☆ ☆ ☆ ☆ ☆

Campground Name: _____

Address: _____

Phone: _____ GPS: _____

Site #: _____ Ideal Site # (for next time): _____

Cost: _____ ☐ day ☐ week ☐ month

Memberships: _____

Altitude: _____ ☐ First Visit ☐ Return Visit

DRIVEWAY LENGTH:

☐ easy access   ☐ back-in   ☐ antenna reception
☐ loop   ☐ pull-through   ☐ satellite tv
☐ paved   ☐ restrooms   ☐ cable tv
☐ unpaved-graded   ☐ pet friendly   ☐ wifi:
☐ picnic table   ☐ shade-partial/full   ☐ free ☐ $____
☐ fire ring   ☐ full sun   **cell phone carrier:**
☐ water   ☐ laundry
☐ sewer   ☐ store/visitor center   _____
☐ electricity   ☐ pool/hot tub   **phone reception**
☐ 15 amp   ☐ hiking trails   ☆ ☆ ☆ ☆ ☆
☐ 30 amp   ☐ fishing   **water pressure**
☐ 50 amp   ☐ firewood   ☆ ☆ ☆ ☆ ☆

NOTES FOR NEXT TIME

(fees, check in/out times, discounts, directions, loud/quiet, etc)

NOTES

(Campground Pros/Cons, Traveling Companions, People Met, Places Visited, Things to Do, Restaurants, Journaling):

RV LOG

DATE: ☀ ⛅ ☁ ☂ ⛈ ❄ 🌫 ☐Hot ☐Cold ☐Mild

Traveled from _____ to _____

Route Taken: _____

Start Mileage: _____ End Mileage: _____ Total Miles Traveled: _____

Sites Along The Way: _____

CAMPGROUND ☆☆☆☆☆

Campground Name: _____

Address: _____

Phone: _____ GPS: _____

Site #: _____ Ideal Site # (for next time): _____

Cost: _____ ☐ day   ☐ week   ☐ month

Memberships: _____

Altitude: _____ ☐ First Visit   ☐ Return Visit

DRIVEWAY LENGTH:

☐easy access   ☐back-in   ☐antenna reception
☐loop   ☐pull-through   ☐satellite tv
☐paved   ☐restrooms   ☐cable tv
☐unpaved-graded   ☐pet friendly   ☐wifi:
☐picnic table   ☐shade-partial/full   ☐free ☐$_____
☐fire ring   ☐full sun   **cell phone carrier:**
☐water   ☐laundry
☐sewer   ☐store/visitor center   _____
☐electricity   ☐pool/hot tub   **phone reception**
☐15 amp   ☐hiking trails   ☆☆☆☆☆
☐30 amp   ☐fishing   **water pressure**
☐50 amp   ☐firewood   ☆☆☆☆☆

NOTES FOR NEXT TIME

(fees, check in/out times, discounts, directions, loud/quiet, etc)

NOTES

(Campground Pros/Cons, Traveling Companions, People Met, Places Visited, Things to Do, Restaurants, Journaling):

RV LOG

DATE: ☼ ⛅ ☁ 🌧 ⛈ ❄ 🌫 ☐ Hot ☐ Cold ☐ Mild

Traveled from _____ to _____

Route Taken: _____

Start Mileage: _____ End Mileage: _____ Total Miles Traveled: _____

Sites Along The Way:

CAMPGROUND ☆☆☆☆☆

Campground Name: _____

Address: _____

Phone: _____ GPS: _____

Site #: _____ Ideal Site # (for next time): _____

Cost: _____ ☐ day ☐ week ☐ month

Memberships: _____

Altitude: _____ ☐ First Visit ☐ Return Visit

DRIVEWAY LENGTH:

☐ easy access ☐ back-in ☐ antenna reception
☐ loop ☐ pull-through ☐ satellite tv
☐ paved ☐ restrooms ☐ cable tv
☐ unpaved-graded ☐ pet friendly ☐ wifi:
☐ picnic table ☐ shade-partial/full ☐ free ☐ $____
☐ fire ring ☐ full sun cell phone carrier:
☐ water ☐ laundry _____
☐ sewer ☐ store/visitor center
☐ electricity ☐ pool/hot tub phone reception
☐ 15 amp ☐ hiking trails ☆☆☆☆☆
☐ 30 amp ☐ fishing water pressure
☐ 50 amp ☐ firewood ☆☆☆☆☆

NOTES FOR NEXT TIME

(fees, check in/out times, discounts, directions, loud/quiet, etc)

NOTES

(Campground Pros/Cons, Traveling Companions, People Met, Places Visited,
Things to Do, Restaurants, Journaling):

RV LOG

DATE: ☀ ⛅ ☁ ☁ ☂ ⛆ ❄ 🌬 ☐Hot ☐Cold ☐Mild

Traveled from _____ to _____

Route Taken: _____

Start Mileage: _____ End Mileage: _____ Total Miles Traveled: _____

Sites Along The Way:

CAMPGROUND ☆☆☆☆☆

Campground Name: _____

Address: _____

Phone: _____ GPS: _____

Site #: _____ Ideal Site # (for next time): _____

Cost: _____ ☐ day   ☐ week   ☐ month

Memberships: _____

Altitude: _____ ☐ First Visit   ☐ Return Visit

DRIVEWAY LENGTH:

☐ easy access   ☐ back-in   ☐ antenna reception
☐ loop   ☐ pull-through   ☐ satellite tv
☐ paved   ☐ restrooms   ☐ cable tv
☐ unpaved-graded ☐ pet friendly   ☐ wifi:
☐ picnic table   ☐ shade-partial/full   ☐ free ☐ $_____
☐ fire ring   ☐ full sun   **cell phone carrier:**
☐ water   ☐ laundry
☐ sewer   ☐ store/visitor center _____
☐ electricity   ☐ pool/hot tub   **phone reception**
☐ 15 amp   ☐ hiking trails   ☆☆☆☆☆
☐ 30 amp   ☐ fishing   **water pressure**
☐ 50 amp   ☐ firewood   ☆☆☆☆☆

NOTES FOR NEXT TIME

(fees, check in/out times, discounts, directions, loud/quiet, etc)

NOTES

(Campground Pros/Cons, Traveling Companions, People Met, Places Visited,
Things to Do, Restaurants, Journaling):

RV LOG

DATE: ☼ ⛅ ☁ 🌧 ⛈ ❄ 🌬 ☐Hot ☐Cold ☐Mild

Traveled from _____ to _____

Route Taken: _____

Start Mileage: _____ End Mileage: _____ Total Miles Traveled: _____

Sites Along The Way: _____

CAMPGROUND ☆☆☆☆☆

Campground Name: _____

Address: _____

Phone: _____ GPS: _____

Site #: _____ Ideal Site # (for next time): _____

Cost: _____ ☐ day ☐ week ☐ month

Memberships: _____

Altitude: _____ ☐ First Visit ☐ Return Visit

DRIVEWAY LENGTH:

☐easy access ☐back-in ☐antenna reception
☐loop ☐pull-through ☐satellite tv
☐paved ☐restrooms ☐cable tv
☐unpaved-graded ☐pet friendly ☐wifi:
☐picnic table ☐shade-partial/full   ☐free ☐$____
☐fire ring ☐full sun
☐water ☐laundry   **cell phone carrier:**
☐sewer ☐store/visitor center
☐electricity ☐pool/hot tub   **phone reception**
☐15 amp ☐hiking trails   ☆☆☆☆☆
☐30 amp ☐fishing   **water pressure**
☐50 amp ☐firewood   ☆☆☆☆☆

NOTES FOR NEXT TIME

(fees, check in/out times, discounts, directions, loud/quiet, etc)

NOTES

(Campground Pros/Cons, Traveling Companions, People Met, Places Visited, Things to Do, Restaurants, Journaling):

RV LOG

DATE: ☀ ⛅ ☁ 🌧 ⚡ ❄ 🌫 ☐Hot ☐Cold ☐Mild

Traveled from _____ to _____

Route Taken: _____

Start Mileage: _____ End Mileage: _____ Total Miles Traveled: _____

Sites Along The Way: _____

CAMPGROUND ☆☆☆☆☆

Campground Name: _____

Address: _____

Phone: _____ GPS: _____

Site #: _____ Ideal Site # (for next time): _____

Cost: _____ ☐ day ☐ week ☐ month

Memberships: _____

Altitude: _____ ☐ First Visit ☐ Return Visit

DRIVEWAY LENGTH:

☐ easy access ☐ back-in ☐ antenna reception
☐ loop ☐ pull-through ☐ satellite tv
☐ paved ☐ restrooms ☐ cable tv
☐ unpaved-graded ☐ pet friendly ☐ wifi:
☐ picnic table ☐ shade-partial/full ☐ free ☐$_____
☐ fire ring ☐ full sun cell phone carrier:
☐ water ☐ laundry
☐ sewer ☐ store/visitor center _____
☐ electricity ☐ pool/hot tub phone reception
☐ 15 amp ☐ hiking trails ☆☆☆☆☆
☐ 30 amp ☐ fishing water pressure
☐ 50 amp ☐ firewood ☆☆☆☆☆

NOTES FOR NEXT TIME

(fees, check in/out times, discounts, directions, loud/quiet, etc)

NOTES

(Campground Pros/Cons, Traveling Companions, People Met, Places Visited,
Things to Do, Restaurants, Journaling):

RV LOG

DATE: ☀ ⛅ ☁ 🌧 🌦 ❄ 🌬 ☐Hot ☐Cold ☐Mild

Traveled from _____ to _____

Route Taken: _____

Start Mileage: _____ End Mileage: _____ Total Miles Traveled: _____

Sites Along The Way: _____

CAMPGROUND ☆☆☆☆☆

Campground Name: _____

Address: _____

Phone: _____ GPS: _____

Site #: _____ Ideal Site # (for next time): _____

Cost: _____ ☐ day ☐ week ☐ month

Memberships: _____

Altitude: _____ ☐ First Visit ☐ Return Visit

DRIVEWAY LENGTH:

☐ easy access
☐ loop
☐ paved
☐ unpaved-graded
☐ picnic table
☐ fire ring
☐ water
☐ sewer
☐ electricity
☐ 15 amp
☐ 30 amp
☐ 50 amp

☐ back-in
☐ pull-through
☐ restrooms
☐ pet friendly
☐ shade-partial/full
☐ full sun
☐ laundry
☐ store/visitor center
☐ pool/hot tub
☐ hiking trails
☐ fishing
☐ firewood

☐ antenna reception
☐ satellite tv
☐ cable tv
☐ wifi:
  ☐ free ☐ $_____

cell phone carrier:

_____

phone reception
☆☆☆☆☆

water pressure
☆☆☆☆☆

NOTES FOR NEXT TIME

(fees, check in/out times, discounts, directions, loud/quiet, etc)

NOTES

(Campground Pros/Cons, Traveling Companions, People Met, Places Visited,
Things to Do, Restaurants, Journaling):

RV   LOG

DATE: ☀ ⛅ ☁ 🌧 ⛈ ❄ 🌫 ☐Hot ☐Cold ☐Mild

Traveled from _____ to _____

Route Taken: _____

Start Mileage: _____ End Mileage: _____ Total Miles Traveled: _____

Sites Along The Way:

CAMPGROUND ☆☆☆☆☆

Campground Name: _____

Address: _____

Phone: _____ GPS: _____

Site #: _____ Ideal Site # (for next time): _____

Cost: _____ ☐ day   ☐ week   ☐ month

Memberships: _____

Altitude: _____ ☐ First Visit   ☐ Return Visit

DRIVEWAY LENGTH:

☐easy access   ☐back-in   ☐antenna reception
☐loop   ☐pull-through   ☐satellite tv
☐paved   ☐restrooms   ☐cable tv
☐unpaved-graded   ☐pet friendly   ☐wifi:
☐picnic table   ☐shade-partial/full   ☐free ☐$____
☐fire ring   ☐full sun   cell phone carrier:
☐water   ☐laundry
☐sewer   ☐store/visitor center   _____
☐electricity   ☐pool/hot tub   phone reception
☐15 amp   ☐hiking trails   ☆☆☆☆☆
☐30 amp   ☐fishing   water pressure
☐50 amp   ☐firewood   ☆☆☆☆☆

NOTES FOR NEXT TIME

(fees, check in/out times, discounts, directions, loud/quiet, etc)

NOTES

(Campground Pros/Cons, Traveling Companions, People Met, Places Visited,
Things to Do, Restaurants, Journaling):

RV LOG

DATE: ☼ ⛅ ☁ 🌧 ⛈ ❄ 🌫 ☐Hot ☐Cold ☐Mild

Traveled from _____ to _____

Route Taken: _____

Start Mileage: _____ End Mileage: _____ Total Miles Traveled: _____

Sites Along The Way: _____

CAMPGROUND ☆☆☆☆☆

Campground Name: _____

Address: _____

Phone: _____ GPS: _____

Site #: _____ Ideal Site # (for next time): _____

Cost: _____ ☐ day ☐ week ☐ month

Memberships: _____

Altitude: _____ ☐ First Visit ☐ Return Visit

DRIVEWAY LENGTH:

☐ easy access   ☐ back-in   ☐ antenna reception
☐ loop   ☐ pull-through   ☐ satellite tv
☐ paved   ☐ restrooms   ☐ cable tv
☐ unpaved-graded   ☐ pet friendly   ☐ wifi:
☐ picnic table   ☐ shade-partial/full   ☐ free ☐ $____
☐ fire ring   ☐ full sun
☐ water   ☐ laundry   **cell phone carrier:**
☐ sewer   ☐ store/visitor center   _____
☐ electricity   ☐ pool/hot tub   **phone reception**
☐ 15 amp   ☐ hiking trails   ☆☆☆☆☆
☐ 30 amp   ☐ fishing   **water pressure**
☐ 50 amp   ☐ firewood   ☆☆☆☆☆

NOTES FOR NEXT TIME

(fees, check in/out times, discounts, directions, loud/quiet, etc)

NOTES

(Campground Pros/Cons, Traveling Companions, People Met, Places Visited,
Things to Do, Restaurants, Journaling):

RV LOG

DATE: ☀ ⛅ ☁ 🌦 🌧 ❄ 🌬 ☐Hot ☐Cold ☐Mild

Traveled from _____ to _____

Route Taken: _____

Start Mileage: _____ End Mileage: _____ Total Miles Traveled: _____

Sites Along The Way:

CAMPGROUND ☆☆☆☆☆

Campground Name: _____

Address: _____

Phone: _____ GPS: _____

Site #: _____ Ideal Site # (for next time): _____

Cost: _____ ☐ day ☐ week ☐ month

Memberships: _____

Altitude: _____ ☐ First Visit ☐ Return Visit

DRIVEWAY LENGTH:

☐easy access   ☐back-in   ☐antenna reception
☐loop   ☐pull-through   ☐satellite tv
☐paved   ☐restrooms   ☐cable tv
☐unpaved-graded   ☐pet friendly   ☐wifi:
☐picnic table   ☐shade-partial/full   ☐free ☐$____
☐fire ring   ☐full sun
☐water   ☐laundry   **cell phone carrier:**
☐sewer   ☐store/visitor center   _____
☐electricity   ☐pool/hot tub   **phone reception**
☐15 amp   ☐hiking trails   ☆☆☆☆☆
☐30 amp   ☐fishing   **water pressure**
☐50 amp   ☐firewood   ☆☆☆☆☆

NOTES FOR NEXT TIME

(fees, check in/out times, discounts, directions, loud/quiet, etc)

NOTES

(Campground Pros/Cons, Traveling Companions, People Met, Places Visited, Things to Do, Restaurants, Journaling):

RV LOG

DATE: ☀ ⛅ ☁ 🌧 ⛈ ❄ 🌫 ☐Hot ☐Cold ☐Mild

Traveled from _____ to _____

Route Taken: _____

Start Mileage: _____ End Mileage: _____ Total Miles Traveled: _____

Sites Along The Way: _____

CAMPGROUND ☆☆☆☆☆

Campground Name: _____

Address: _____

Phone: _____ GPS: _____

Site #: _____ Ideal Site # (for next time): _____

Cost: _____ ☐ day ☐ week ☐ month

Memberships: _____

Altitude: _____ ☐ First Visit ☐ Return Visit

DRIVEWAY LENGTH:

☐easy access   ☐back-in   ☐antenna reception
☐loop   ☐pull-through   ☐satellite tv
☐paved   ☐restrooms   ☐cable tv
☐unpaved-graded   ☐pet friendly   ☐wifi:
☐picnic table   ☐shade-partial/full   ☐free ☐$_____
☐fire ring   ☐full sun   cell phone carrier:
☐water   ☐laundry
☐sewer   ☐store/visitor center _____
☐electricity   ☐pool/hot tub   phone reception
☐15 amp   ☐hiking trails   ☆☆☆☆☆
☐30 amp   ☐fishing   water pressure
☐50 amp   ☐firewood   ☆☆☆☆☆

NOTES FOR NEXT TIME

(fees, check in/out times, discounts, directions, loud/quiet, etc)

NOTES

(Campground Pros/Cons, Traveling Companions, People Met, Places Visited, Things to Do, Restaurants, Journaling):

RV LOG

DATE: ☀ ⛅ ☁ 🌧 ⛈ ❄ 🌫 ☐Hot ☐Cold ☐Mild

Traveled from _____ to _____

Route Taken: _____

Start Mileage: _____ End Mileage: _____ Total Miles Traveled: _____

Sites Along The Way: _____

CAMPGROUND ☆☆☆☆☆

Campground Name: _____

Address: _____

Phone: _____ GPS: _____

Site #: _____ Ideal Site # (for next time): _____

Cost: _____ ☐ day ☐ week ☐ month

Memberships: _____

Altitude: _____ ☐ First Visit ☐ Return Visit

DRIVEWAY LENGTH:

☐easy access   ☐back-in   ☐antenna reception
☐loop   ☐pull-through   ☐satellite tv
☐paved   ☐restrooms   ☐cable tv
☐unpaved-graded   ☐pet friendly   ☐wifi:
☐picnic table   ☐shade-partial/full   ☐free ☐$____
☐fire ring   ☐full sun   cell phone carrier:
☐water   ☐laundry
☐sewer   ☐store/visitor center   _____
☐electricity   ☐pool/hot tub   phone reception
☐15 amp   ☐hiking trails   ☆☆☆☆☆
☐30 amp   ☐fishing   water pressure
☐50 amp   ☐firewood   ☆☆☆☆☆

NOTES FOR NEXT TIME

(fees, check in/out times, discounts, directions, loud/quiet, etc)

NOTES

(Campground Pros/Cons, Traveling Companions, People Met, Places Visited,
Things to Do, Restaurants, Journaling):

RV   LOG

DATE: ☀ ⛅ ☁ 🌧 ⛈ ❄ 🌬 ☐Hot ☐Cold ☐Mild

Traveled from _____ to _____

Route Taken: _____

Start Mileage: _____ End Mileage: _____ Total Miles Traveled: _____

Sites Along The Way:

CAMPGROUND ☆☆☆☆☆

Campground Name: _____

Address: _____

Phone: _____ GPS: _____

Site #: _____ Ideal Site # (for next time): _____

Cost: _____ ☐ day ☐ week ☐ month

Memberships: _____

Altitude: _____ ☐ First Visit ☐ Return Visit

DRIVEWAY LENGTH:

☐easy access ☐back-in ☐antenna reception
☐loop ☐pull-through ☐satellite tv
☐paved ☐restrooms ☐cable tv
☐unpaved-graded ☐pet friendly ☐wifi:
☐picnic table ☐shade-partial/full   ☐free ☐$____
☐fire ring ☐full sun   cell phone carrier:
☐water ☐laundry
☐sewer ☐store/visitor center _____
☐electricity ☐pool/hot tub   phone reception
☐15 amp ☐hiking trails ☆☆☆☆☆
☐30 amp ☐fishing   water pressure
☐50 amp ☐firewood ☆☆☆☆☆

NOTES FOR NEXT TIME

(fees, check in/out times, discounts, directions, loud/quiet, etc)

NOTES

(Campground Pros/Cons, Traveling Companions, People Met, Places Visited, Things to Do, Restaurants, Journaling):

RV LOG

DATE: ☀ ⛅ ☁ 🌧 ⛈ ❄ 🌬 ☐Hot ☐Cold ☐Mild

Traveled from _____ to _____

Route Taken: _____

Start Mileage: _____ End Mileage: _____ Total Miles Traveled: _____

Sites Along The Way: _____

CAMPGROUND ☆☆☆☆☆

Campground Name: _____

Address: _____

Phone: _____ GPS: _____

Site #: _____ Ideal Site # (for next time): _____

Cost: _____ ☐ day ☐ week ☐ month

Memberships: _____

Altitude: _____ ☐ First Visit ☐ Return Visit

DRIVEWAY LENGTH:

☐easy access ☐back-in ☐antenna reception
☐loop ☐pull-through ☐satellite tv
☐paved ☐restrooms ☐cable tv
☐unpaved-graded ☐pet friendly ☐wifi:
☐picnic table ☐shade-partial/full ☐free ☐$____
☐fire ring ☐full sun cell phone carrier:
☐water ☐laundry
☐sewer ☐store/visitor center _____
☐electricity ☐pool/hot tub phone reception
☐15 amp ☐hiking trails ☆☆☆☆☆
☐30 amp ☐fishing water pressure
☐50 amp ☐firewood ☆☆☆☆☆

NOTES FOR NEXT TIME

(fees, check in/out times, discounts, directions, loud/quiet, etc)

NOTES

(Campground Pros/Cons, Traveling Companions, People Met, Places Visited, Things to Do, Restaurants, Journaling):

RV LOG

DATE: ☀ ⛅ ☁ 🌧 ⛈ ❄ 🌬 ☐Hot ☐Cold ☐Mild

Traveled from _____ to _____

Route Taken: _____

Start Mileage: _____ End Mileage: _____ Total Miles Traveled: _____

Sites Along The Way: _____

CAMPGROUND ☆☆☆☆☆

Campground Name: _____

Address: _____

Phone: _____ GPS: _____

Site #: _____ Ideal Site # (for next time): _____

Cost: _____ ☐ day ☐ week ☐ month

Memberships: _____

Altitude: _____ ☐ First Visit ☐ Return Visit

DRIVEWAY LENGTH:

☐ easy access
☐ loop
☐ paved
☐ unpaved-graded
☐ picnic table
☐ fire ring
☐ water
☐ sewer
☐ electricity
☐ 15 amp
☐ 30 amp
☐ 50 amp

☐ back-in
☐ pull-through
☐ restrooms
☐ pet friendly
☐ shade-partial/full
☐ full sun
☐ laundry
☐ store/visitor center
☐ pool/hot tub
☐ hiking trails
☐ fishing
☐ firewood

☐ antenna reception
☐ satellite tv
☐ cable tv
☐ wifi:
  ☐ free ☐ $_____

cell phone carrier:
_____

phone reception
☆☆☆☆☆

water pressure
☆☆☆☆☆

NOTES FOR NEXT TIME

(fees, check in/out times, discounts, directions, loud/quiet, etc)

NOTES

(Campground Pros/Cons, Traveling Companions, People Met, Places Visited,
Things to Do, Restaurants, Journaling):

RV LOG

DATE: ☀ ⛅ ☁ ☔ ⛈ ❄ 🌫 ☐Hot ☐Cold ☐Mild

Traveled from _____ to _____

Route Taken: _____

Start Mileage: _____ End Mileage: _____ Total Miles Traveled: _____

Sites Along The Way:

CAMPGROUND   ☆☆☆☆☆

Campground Name: _____

Address: _____

Phone: _____ GPS: _____

Site #: _____ Ideal Site # (for next time): _____

Cost: _____ ☐ day ☐ week ☐ month

Memberships: _____

Altitude: _____ ☐ First Visit   ☐ Return Visit

DRIVEWAY LENGTH:

☐ easy access
☐ loop
☐ paved
☐ unpaved-graded
☐ picnic table
☐ fire ring
☐ water
☐ sewer
☐ electricity
☐ 15 amp
☐ 30 amp
☐ 50 amp

☐ back-in
☐ pull-through
☐ restrooms
☐ pet friendly
☐ shade-partial/full
☐ full sun
☐ laundry
☐ store/visitor center
☐ pool/hot tub
☐ hiking trails
☐ fishing
☐ firewood

☐ antenna reception
☐ satellite tv
☐ cable tv
☐ wifi:
   ☐ free ☐ $_____

cell phone carrier:
_____

phone reception
☆☆☆☆☆
water pressure
☆☆☆☆☆

NOTES FOR NEXT TIME

(fees, check in/out times, discounts, directions, loud/quiet, etc)

NOTES

(Campground Pros/Cons, Traveling Companions, People Met, Places Visited,
Things to Do, Restaurants, Journaling):

RV · LOG

DATE: ☀ ⛅ ☁ 🌧 ⛈ ❄ 🌫 ☐Hot ☐Cold ☐Mild

Traveled from _____ to _____

Route Taken: _____

Start Mileage: _____ End Mileage: _____ Total Miles Traveled: _____

Sites Along The Way:

CAMPGROUND ☆☆☆☆☆

Campground Name: _____

Address: _____

Phone: _____ GPS: _____

Site #: _____ Ideal Site # (for next time): _____

Cost: _____ ☐ day ☐ week ☐ month

Memberships: _____

Altitude: _____ ☐ First Visit ☐ Return Visit

DRIVEWAY LENGTH:

☐ easy access   ☐ back-in   ☐ antenna reception
☐ loop   ☐ pull-through   ☐ satellite tv
☐ paved   ☐ restrooms   ☐ cable tv
☐ unpaved-graded   ☐ pet friendly   ☐ wifi:
☐ picnic table   ☐ shade-partial/full   ☐ free ☐ $____
☐ fire ring   ☐ full sun   **cell phone carrier:**
☐ water   ☐ laundry
☐ sewer   ☐ store/visitor center _____
☐ electricity   ☐ pool/hot tub   **phone reception**
☐ 15 amp   ☐ hiking trails   ☆☆☆☆☆
☐ 30 amp   ☐ fishing   **water pressure**
☐ 50 amp   ☐ firewood   ☆☆☆☆☆

NOTES FOR NEXT TIME

(fees, check in/out times, discounts, directions, loud/quiet, etc)

NOTES

(Campground Pros/Cons, Traveling Companions, People Met, Places Visited, Things to Do, Restaurants, Journaling):

RV LOG

DATE: ☀ ⛅ ☁ 🌧 ⛈ ❄ 🌫 ☐Hot ☐Cold ☐Mild

Traveled from _____ to _____

Route Taken: _____

Start Mileage: _____ End Mileage: _____ Total Miles Traveled: _____

Sites Along The Way: _____

CAMPGROUND ☆☆☆☆☆

Campground Name: _____

Address: _____

Phone: _____ GPS: _____

Site #: _____ Ideal Site # (for next time): _____

Cost: _____ ☐ day ☐ week ☐ month

Memberships: _____

Altitude: _____ ☐ First Visit ☐ Return Visit

DRIVEWAY LENGTH:

☐ easy access ☐ back-in ☐ antenna reception
☐ loop ☐ pull-through ☐ satellite tv
☐ paved ☐ restrooms ☐ cable tv
☐ unpaved-graded ☐ pet friendly ☐ wifi:
☐ picnic table ☐ shade-partial/full   ☐ free ☐ $_____
☐ fire ring ☐ full sun   cell phone carrier:
☐ water ☐ laundry
☐ sewer ☐ store/visitor center   _____
☐ electricity ☐ pool/hot tub   phone reception
☐ 15 amp ☐ hiking trails   ☆☆☆☆☆
☐ 30 amp ☐ fishing   water pressure
☐ 50 amp ☐ firewood   ☆☆☆☆☆

NOTES FOR NEXT TIME

(fees, check in/out times, discounts, directions, loud/quiet, etc)

NOTES

(Campground Pros/Cons, Traveling Companions, People Met, Places Visited, Things to Do, Restaurants, Journaling):

RV LOG

DATE: ☀️ ⛅ ☁️ 🌧️ ⛈️ ❄️ 🌬️ ☐Hot ☐Cold ☐Mild

Traveled from _____ to _____

Route Taken: _____

Start Mileage: _____ End Mileage: _____ Total Miles Traveled: _____

Sites Along The Way: _____

CAMPGROUND ☆☆☆☆☆

Campground Name: _____

Address: _____

Phone: _____ GPS: _____

Site #: _____ Ideal Site # (for next time): _____

Cost: _____ ☐ day ☐ week ☐ month

Memberships: _____

Altitude: _____ ☐ First Visit ☐ Return Visit

DRIVEWAY LENGTH:

☐easy access ☐back-in ☐antenna reception
☐loop ☐pull-through ☐satellite tv
☐paved ☐restrooms ☐cable tv
☐unpaved-graded ☐pet friendly ☐wifi:
☐picnic table ☐shade-partial/full   ☐free ☐$____
☐fire ring ☐full sun
☐water ☐laundry   cell phone carrier:
☐sewer ☐store/visitor center
☐electricity ☐pool/hot tub _____
☐15 amp ☐hiking trails   phone reception
☐30 amp ☐fishing ☆☆☆☆☆
☐50 amp ☐firewood   water pressure
  ☆☆☆☆☆

NOTES FOR NEXT TIME

(fees, check in/out times, discounts, directions, loud/quiet, etc)

NOTES

(Campground Pros/Cons, Traveling Companions, People Met, Places Visited,
Things to Do, Restaurants, Journaling):

RV LOG

DATE: ☀ ⛅ ☁ 🌧 ⛈ ❄ 🌫 ☐Hot ☐Cold ☐Mild

Traveled from _____ to _____

Route Taken: _____

Start Mileage: _____ End Mileage: _____ Total Miles Traveled: _____

Sites Along The Way: _____

CAMPGROUND ☆☆☆☆☆

Campground Name: _____

Address: _____

Phone: _____ GPS: _____

Site #: _____ Ideal Site # (for next time): _____

Cost: _____ ☐ day ☐ week ☐ month

Memberships: _____

Altitude: _____ ☐ First Visit ☐ Return Visit

DRIVEWAY LENGTH:

☐ easy access
☐ loop
☐ paved
☐ unpaved-graded
☐ picnic table
☐ fire ring
☐ water
☐ sewer
☐ electricity
☐ 15 amp
☐ 30 amp
☐ 50 amp

☐ back-in
☐ pull-through
☐ restrooms
☐ pet friendly
☐ shade-partial/full
☐ full sun
☐ laundry
☐ store/visitor center
☐ pool/hot tub
☐ hiking trails
☐ fishing
☐ firewood

☐ antenna reception
☐ satellite tv
☐ cable tv
☐ wifi:
  ☐ free ☐ $_____

cell phone carrier:
_____

phone reception
☆☆☆☆☆

water pressure
☆☆☆☆☆

NOTES FOR NEXT TIME

(fees, check in/out times, discounts, directions, loud/quiet, etc)

NOTES

(Campground Pros/Cons, Traveling Companions, People Met, Places Visited,
Things to Do, Restaurants, Journaling):

RV LOG

DATE: ☀ ⛅ ☁ 🌧 ⛈ ❄ 🌫 ☐Hot ☐Cold ☐Mild

Traveled from _____ to _____

Route Taken: _____

Start Mileage: _____ End Mileage: _____ Total Miles Traveled: _____

Sites Along The Way: _____

CAMPGROUND ☆☆☆☆☆

Campground Name: _____

Address: _____

Phone: _____ GPS: _____

Site #: _____ Ideal Site # (for next time): _____

Cost: _____ ☐ day ☐ week ☐ month

Memberships: _____

Altitude: _____ ☐ First Visit ☐ Return Visit

DRIVEWAY LENGTH:

☐ easy access   ☐ back-in   ☐ antenna reception
☐ loop   ☐ pull-through   ☐ satellite tv
☐ paved   ☐ restrooms   ☐ cable tv
☐ unpaved-graded   ☐ pet friendly   ☐ wifi:
☐ picnic table   ☐ shade-partial/full   ☐ free ☐$____
☐ fire ring   ☐ full sun   cell phone carrier:
☐ water   ☐ laundry
☐ sewer   ☐ store/visitor center   _____
☐ electricity   ☐ pool/hot tub   phone reception
☐ 15 amp   ☐ hiking trails   ☆☆☆☆☆
☐ 30 amp   ☐ fishing   water pressure
☐ 50 amp   ☐ firewood   ☆☆☆☆☆

NOTES FOR NEXT TIME

(fees, check in/out times, discounts, directions, loud/quiet, etc)

NOTES

(Campground Pros/Cons, Traveling Companions, People Met, Places Visited, Things to Do, Restaurants, Journaling):

RV LOG

DATE: ☀ ⛅ ☁ ☂ ⛈ ❄ 🌬 ☐Hot ☐Cold ☐Mild

Traveled from _____ to _____

Route Taken: _____

Start Mileage: _____ End Mileage: _____ Total Miles Traveled: _____

Sites Along The Way:

CAMPGROUND ☆☆☆☆☆

Campground Name: _____

Address: _____

Phone: _____ GPS: _____

Site #: _____ Ideal Site # (for next time): _____

Cost: _____ ☐ day ☐ week ☐ month

Memberships: _____

Altitude: _____ ☐ First Visit ☐ Return Visit

DRIVEWAY LENGTH:

☐easy access	☐back-in	☐antenna reception
☐loop	☐pull-through	☐satellite tv
☐paved	☐restrooms	☐cable tv
☐unpaved-graded	☐pet friendly	☐wifi:
☐picnic table	☐shade-partial/full	☐free ☐$____
☐fire ring	☐full sun	cell phone carrier:
☐water	☐laundry	
☐sewer	☐store/visitor center	_____
☐electricity	☐pool/hot tub	phone reception
☐15 amp	☐hiking trails	☆☆☆☆☆
☐30 amp	☐fishing	water pressure
☐50 amp	☐firewood	☆☆☆☆☆

NOTES FOR NEXT TIME

(fees, check in/out times, discounts, directions, loud/quiet, etc)

NOTES

(Campground Pros/Cons, Traveling Companions, People Met, Places Visited,
Things to Do, Restaurants, Journaling):

RV LOG

DATE: ☀️ ⛅ ☁️ 🌧️ ⛈️ ❄️ 🌫️ ☐Hot ☐Cold ☐Mild

Traveled from _____ to _____

Route Taken: _____

Start Mileage: _____ End Mileage: _____ Total Miles Traveled: _____

Sites Along The Way: _____

CAMPGROUND ☆☆☆☆☆

Campground Name: _____

Address: _____

Phone: _____ GPS: _____

Site #: _____ Ideal Site # (for next time): _____

Cost: _____ ☐ day ☐ week ☐ month

Memberships: _____

Altitude: _____ ☐ First Visit ☐ Return Visit

DRIVEWAY LENGTH:

☐easy access   ☐back-in   ☐antenna reception
☐loop   ☐pull-through   ☐satellite tv
☐paved   ☐restrooms   ☐cable tv
☐unpaved-graded   ☐pet friendly   ☐wifi:
☐picnic table   ☐shade-partial/full   ☐free ☐$_____
☐fire ring   ☐full sun   cell phone carrier:
☐water   ☐laundry
☐sewer   ☐store/visitor center _____
☐electricity   ☐pool/hot tub   phone reception
☐15 amp   ☐hiking trails   ☆☆☆☆☆
☐30 amp   ☐fishing   water pressure
☐50 amp   ☐firewood   ☆☆☆☆☆

NOTES FOR NEXT TIME

(fees, check in/out times, discounts, directions, loud/quiet, etc)

NOTES

(Campground Pros/Cons, Traveling Companions, People Met, Places Visited, Things to Do, Restaurants, Journaling):

RV LOG

DATE: ☀️ ⛅ ☁️ 🌧️ 🌦️ ❄️ 🌫️ ☐Hot ☐Cold ☐Mild

Traveled from _____ to _____

Route Taken: _____

Start Mileage: _____ End Mileage: _____ Total Miles Traveled: _____

Sites Along The Way:

CAMPGROUND ☆☆☆☆☆

Campground Name: _____

Address: _____

Phone: _____ GPS: _____

Site #: _____ Ideal Site # (for next time): _____

Cost: _____ ☐ day ☐ week ☐ month

Memberships: _____

Altitude: _____ ☐ First Visit ☐ Return Visit

DRIVEWAY LENGTH:

☐ easy access   ☐ back-in   ☐ antenna reception
☐ loop   ☐ pull-through   ☐ satellite tv
☐ paved   ☐ restrooms   ☐ cable tv
☐ unpaved-graded   ☐ pet friendly   ☐ wifi:
☐ picnic table   ☐ shade-partial/full   ☐ free ☐ $_____
☐ fire ring   ☐ full sun   **cell phone carrier:**
☐ water   ☐ laundry
☐ sewer   ☐ store/visitor center   _____
☐ electricity   ☐ pool/hot tub   **phone reception**
☐ 15 amp   ☐ hiking trails   ☆☆☆☆☆
☐ 30 amp   ☐ fishing   **water pressure**
☐ 50 amp   ☐ firewood   ☆☆☆☆☆

NOTES FOR NEXT TIME

(fees, check in/out times, discounts, directions, loud/quiet, etc)

NOTES

(Campground Pros/Cons, Traveling Companions, People Met, Places Visited,
Things to Do, Restaurants, Journaling):

RV LOG

DATE: ☀ ⛅ ☁ ☂ 🌧 ❄ 🌫 ☐Hot ☐Cold ☐Mild

Traveled from _____ to _____

Route Taken: _____

Start Mileage: _____ End Mileage: _____ Total Miles Traveled: _____

Sites Along The Way: _____

CAMPGROUND ☆☆☆☆☆

Campground Name: _____

Address: _____

Phone: _____ GPS: _____

Site #: _____ Ideal Site # (for next time): _____

Cost: _____ ☐ day ☐ week ☐ month

Memberships: _____

Altitude: _____ ☐ First Visit ☐ Return Visit

DRIVEWAY LENGTH:

☐ easy access   ☐ back-in   ☐ antenna reception
☐ loop   ☐ pull-through   ☐ satellite tv
☐ paved   ☐ restrooms   ☐ cable tv
☐ unpaved-graded ☐ pet friendly   ☐ wifi:
☐ picnic table   ☐ shade-partial/full   ☐ free ☐ $____
☐ fire ring   ☐ full sun   cell phone carrier:
☐ water   ☐ laundry
☐ sewer   ☐ store/visitor center   _____
☐ electricity   ☐ pool/hot tub   phone reception
☐ 15 amp   ☐ hiking trails   ☆☆☆☆☆
☐ 30 amp   ☐ fishing   water pressure
☐ 50 amp   ☐ firewood   ☆☆☆☆☆

NOTES FOR NEXT TIME

(fees, check in/out times, discounts, directions, loud/quiet, etc)

NOTES

(Campground Pros/Cons, Traveling Companions, People Met, Places Visited,
Things to Do, Restaurants, Journaling):

RV LOG

DATE: ☀️ ⛅ ☁️ 🌧️ ⛈️ ❄️ 🌫️ ☐Hot ☐Cold ☐Mild

Traveled from _____ to _____

Route Taken: _____

Start Mileage: _____ End Mileage: _____ Total Miles Traveled: _____

Sites Along The Way: _____

CAMPGROUND ☆☆☆☆☆

Campground Name: _____

Address: _____

Phone: _____ GPS: _____

Site #: _____ Ideal Site # (for next time): _____

Cost: _____ ☐ day ☐ week ☐ month

Memberships: _____

Altitude: _____ ☐ First Visit ☐ Return Visit

DRIVEWAY LENGTH:

☐easy access	☐back-in	☐antenna reception
☐loop	☐pull-through	☐satellite tv
☐paved	☐restrooms	☐cable tv
☐unpaved-graded	☐pet friendly	☐wifi:
☐picnic table	☐shade-partial/full	☐free ☐$_____
☐fire ring	☐full sun	cell phone carrier:
☐water	☐laundry	
☐sewer	☐store/visitor center	_____
☐electricity	☐pool/hot tub	phone reception
☐15 amp	☐hiking trails	☆☆☆☆☆
☐30 amp	☐fishing	water pressure
☐50 amp	☐firewood	☆☆☆☆☆

NOTES FOR NEXT TIME

(fees, check in/out times, discounts, directions, loud/quiet, etc)

NOTES

(Campground Pros/Cons, Traveling Companions, People Met, Places Visited,
Things to Do, Restaurants, Journaling):

RV LOG

DATE: ☀ ⛅ ☁ 🌧 ⛈ ❄ 🌫 ☐Hot ☐Cold ☐Mild

Traveled from _____ to _____

Route Taken: _____

Start Mileage: _____ End Mileage: _____ Total Miles Traveled: _____

Sites Along The Way: _____

CAMPGROUND ☆☆☆☆☆

Campground Name: _____

Address: _____

Phone: _____ GPS: _____

Site #: _____ Ideal Site # (for next time): _____

Cost: _____ ☐ day ☐ week ☐ month

Memberships: _____

Altitude: _____ ☐ First Visit ☐ Return Visit

DRIVEWAY LENGTH:

☐easy access
☐loop
☐paved
☐unpaved-graded
☐picnic table
☐fire ring
☐water
☐sewer
☐electricity
☐15 amp
☐30 amp
☐50 amp

☐back-in
☐pull-through
☐restrooms
☐pet friendly
☐shade-partial/full
☐full sun
☐laundry
☐store/visitor center
☐pool/hot tub
☐hiking trails
☐fishing
☐firewood

☐antenna reception
☐satellite tv
☐cable tv
☐wifi:
  ☐free ☐$_____
cell phone carrier:

_____

phone reception
☆☆☆☆☆
water pressure
☆☆☆☆☆

NOTES FOR NEXT TIME

(fees, check in/out times, discounts, directions, loud/quiet, etc)

NOTES

(Campground Pros/Cons, Traveling Companions, People Met, Places Visited, Things to Do, Restaurants, Journaling):

RV LOG

DATE: ☀ ⛅ ☁ 🌧 ⛈ ❄ 🌬 ☐Hot ☐Cold ☐Mild

Traveled from _____ to _____

Route Taken: _____

Start Mileage: _____ End Mileage: _____ Total Miles Traveled: _____

Sites Along The Way:

CAMPGROUND ☆☆☆☆☆

Campground Name: _____

Address: _____

Phone: _____ GPS: _____

Site #: _____ Ideal Site # (for next time): _____

Cost: _____ ☐ day ☐ week ☐ month

Memberships: _____

Altitude: _____ ☐ First Visit ☐ Return Visit

DRIVEWAY LENGTH:

☐easy access ☐back-in ☐antenna reception
☐loop ☐pull-through ☐satellite tv
☐paved ☐restrooms ☐cable tv
☐unpaved-graded ☐pet friendly ☐wifi:
☐picnic table ☐shade-partial/full ☐free ☐$____
☐fire ring ☐full sun cell phone carrier:
☐water ☐laundry
☐sewer ☐store/visitor center _____
☐electricity ☐pool/hot tub phone reception
☐15 amp ☐hiking trails ☆☆☆☆☆
☐30 amp ☐fishing water pressure
☐50 amp ☐firewood ☆☆☆☆☆

NOTES FOR NEXT TIME

(fees, check in/out times, discounts, directions, loud/quiet, etc)

NOTES

(Campground Pros/Cons, Traveling Companions, People Met, Places Visited, Things to Do, Restaurants, Journaling):

RV LOG

DATE: ☀ ⛅ ☁ 🌧 ⛈ ❄ 🌫 ☐Hot ☐Cold ☐Mild

Traveled from _____ to _____

Route Taken: _____

Start Mileage: _____ End Mileage: _____ Total Miles Traveled: _____

Sites Along The Way: _____

CAMPGROUND ☆☆☆☆☆

Campground Name: _____

Address: _____

Phone: _____ GPS: _____

Site #: _____ Ideal Site # (for next time): _____

Cost: _____ ☐ day ☐ week ☐ month

Memberships: _____

Altitude: _____ ☐ First Visit ☐ Return Visit

DRIVEWAY LENGTH:

☐ easy access   ☐ back-in   ☐ antenna reception
☐ loop   ☐ pull-through   ☐ satellite tv
☐ paved   ☐ restrooms   ☐ cable tv
☐ unpaved-graded ☐ pet friendly   ☐ wifi:
☐ picnic table   ☐ shade-partial/full   ☐ free ☐ $____
☐ fire ring   ☐ full sun   cell phone carrier:
☐ water   ☐ laundry
☐ sewer   ☐ store/visitor center   _____
☐ electricity   ☐ pool/hot tub   phone reception
☐ 15 amp   ☐ hiking trails   ☆☆☆☆☆
☐ 30 amp   ☐ fishing   water pressure
☐ 50 amp   ☐ firewood   ☆☆☆☆☆

NOTES FOR NEXT TIME

(fees, check in/out times, discounts, directions, loud/quiet, etc)

NOTES

(Campground Pros/Cons, Traveling Companions, People Met, Places Visited, Things to Do, Restaurants, Journaling):

RV LOG

DATE: ☀ ⛅ ☁ 🌧 ⛈ ❄ 🌫 ☐Hot ☐Cold ☐Mild

Traveled from _____ to _____

Route Taken: _____

Start Mileage: _____ End Mileage: _____ Total Miles Traveled: _____

Sites Along The Way: _____

CAMPGROUND ☆☆☆☆☆

Campground Name: _____

Address: _____

Phone: _____ GPS: _____

Site #: _____ Ideal Site # (for next time): _____

Cost: _____ ☐ day ☐ week ☐ month

Memberships: _____

Altitude: _____ ☐ First Visit ☐ Return Visit

DRIVEWAY LENGTH:

☐easy access	☐back-in	☐antenna reception
☐loop	☐pull-through	☐satellite tv
☐paved	☐restrooms	☐cable tv
☐unpaved-graded	☐pet friendly	☐wifi:
☐picnic table	☐shade-partial/full	☐free ☐$_____
☐fire ring	☐full sun	cell phone carrier:
☐water	☐laundry	
☐sewer	☐store/visitor center	_____
☐electricity	☐pool/hot tub	phone reception
☐15 amp	☐hiking trails	☆☆☆☆☆
☐30 amp	☐fishing	water pressure
☐50 amp	☐firewood	☆☆☆☆☆

NOTES FOR NEXT TIME

(fees, check in/out times, discounts, directions, loud/quiet, etc)

NOTES

(Campground Pros/Cons, Traveling Companions, People Met, Places Visited, Things to Do, Restaurants, Journaling):

RV LOG

DATE: ☀ ⛅ ☁ 🌧 ⛈ ❄ 🌬 ☐ Hot ☐ Cold ☐ Mild

Traveled from _____ to _____

Route Taken: _____

Start Mileage: _____ End Mileage: _____ Total Miles Traveled: _____

Sites Along The Way: _____

CAMPGROUND ☆☆☆☆☆

Campground Name: _____

Address: _____

Phone: _____ GPS: _____

Site #: _____ Ideal Site # (for next time): _____

Cost: _____ ☐ day ☐ week ☐ month

Memberships: _____

Altitude: _____ ☐ First Visit ☐ Return Visit

DRIVEWAY LENGTH:

☐ easy access   ☐ back-in   ☐ antenna reception
☐ loop   ☐ pull-through   ☐ satellite tv
☐ paved   ☐ restrooms   ☐ cable tv
☐ unpaved-graded   ☐ pet friendly   ☐ wifi:
☐ picnic table   ☐ shade-partial/full   ☐ free ☐ $_____
☐ fire ring   ☐ full sun
☐ water   ☐ laundry   **cell phone carrier:**
☐ sewer   ☐ store/visitor center
☐ electricity   ☐ pool/hot tub   **phone reception**
☐ 15 amp   ☐ hiking trails   ☆☆☆☆☆
☐ 30 amp   ☐ fishing   **water pressure**
☐ 50 amp   ☐ firewood   ☆☆☆☆☆

NOTES FOR NEXT TIME

(fees, check in/out times, discounts, directions, loud/quiet, etc)

NOTES

(Campground Pros/Cons, Traveling Companions, People Met, Places Visited, Things to Do, Restaurants, Journaling):

RV LOG

DATE: ☀ ⛅ ☁ 🌧 ⛈ ❄ 🌫 ☐Hot ☐Cold ☐Mild

Traveled from _____ to _____

Route Taken: _____

Start Mileage: _____ End Mileage: _____ Total Miles Traveled: _____

Sites Along The Way:

CAMPGROUND ☆☆☆☆☆

Campground Name: _____

Address: _____

Phone: _____ GPS: _____

Site #: _____ Ideal Site # (for next time): _____

Cost: _____ ☐ day ☐ week ☐ month

Memberships: _____

Altitude: _____ ☐ First Visit ☐ Return Visit

DRIVEWAY LENGTH:

☐ easy access   ☐ back-in   ☐ antenna reception
☐ loop   ☐ pull-through   ☐ satellite tv
☐ paved   ☐ restrooms   ☐ cable tv
☐ unpaved-graded   ☐ pet friendly   ☐ wifi:
☐ picnic table   ☐ shade-partial/full   ☐ free ☐ $____
☐ fire ring   ☐ full sun
☐ water   ☐ laundry   cell phone carrier:
☐ sewer   ☐ store/visitor center
☐ electricity   ☐ pool/hot tub   phone reception
☐ 15 amp   ☐ hiking trails   ☆☆☆☆☆
☐ 30 amp   ☐ fishing   water pressure
☐ 50 amp   ☐ firewood   ☆☆☆☆☆

NOTES FOR NEXT TIME

(fees, check in/out times, discounts, directions, loud/quiet, etc)

NOTES

(Campground Pros/Cons, Traveling Companions, People Met, Places Visited, Things to Do, Restaurants, Journaling):

RV LOG

DATE: ☀ ⛅ ☁ 🌧 ⛈ ❄ 🌫 ☐ Hot ☐ Cold ☐ Mild

Traveled from _____ to _____

Route Taken: _____

Start Mileage: _____ End Mileage: _____ Total Miles Traveled: _____

Sites Along The Way: _____

CAMPGROUND ☆☆☆☆☆

Campground Name: _____

Address: _____

Phone: _____ GPS: _____

Site #: _____ Ideal Site # (for next time): _____

Cost: _____ ☐ day ☐ week ☐ month

Memberships: _____

Altitude: _____ ☐ First Visit ☐ Return Visit

DRIVEWAY LENGTH:

☐ easy access ☐ back-in ☐ antenna reception
☐ loop ☐ pull-through ☐ satellite tv
☐ paved ☐ restrooms ☐ cable tv
☐ unpaved-graded ☐ pet friendly ☐ wifi:
☐ picnic table ☐ shade-partial/full   ☐ free ☐ $_____
☐ fire ring ☐ full sun
☐ water ☐ laundry   **cell phone carrier:**
☐ sewer ☐ store/visitor center _____
☐ electricity ☐ pool/hot tub **phone reception**
☐ 15 amp ☐ hiking trails ☆☆☆☆☆
☐ 30 amp ☐ fishing **water pressure**
☐ 50 amp ☐ firewood ☆☆☆☆☆

NOTES FOR NEXT TIME

(fees, check in/out times, discounts, directions, loud/quiet, etc)

NOTES

(Campground Pros/Cons, Traveling Companions, People Met, Places Visited,
Things to Do, Restaurants, Journaling):

RV LOG

DATE: ☀ ⛅ ☁ 🌧 ⛈ ❄ 🌫 ☐Hot ☐Cold ☐Mild

Traveled from _____ to _____

Route Taken: _____

Start Mileage: _____ End Mileage: _____ Total Miles Traveled: _____

Sites Along The Way: _____

CAMPGROUND ☆☆☆☆☆

Campground Name: _____

Address: _____

Phone: _____ GPS: _____

Site #: _____ Ideal Site # (for next time): _____

Cost: _____ ☐ day ☐ week ☐ month

Memberships: _____

Altitude: _____ ☐ First Visit ☐ Return Visit

DRIVEWAY LENGTH:

☐ easy access
☐ loop
☐ paved
☐ unpaved-graded
☐ picnic table
☐ fire ring
☐ water
☐ sewer
☐ electricity
☐ 15 amp
☐ 30 amp
☐ 50 amp

☐ back-in
☐ pull-through
☐ restrooms
☐ pet friendly
☐ shade-partial/full
☐ full sun
☐ laundry
☐ store/visitor center
☐ pool/hot tub
☐ hiking trails
☐ fishing
☐ firewood

☐ antenna reception
☐ satellite tv
☐ cable tv
☐ wifi:
   ☐ free ☐ $_____

cell phone carrier:

_____

phone reception
☆☆☆☆☆

water pressure
☆☆☆☆☆

NOTES FOR NEXT TIME

(fees, check in/out times, discounts, directions, loud/quiet, etc)

NOTES

(Campground Pros/Cons, Traveling Companions, People Met, Places Visited, Things to Do, Restaurants, Journaling):

RV LOG

DATE: ☀ ⛅ ☁ 🌧 ⛈ ❄ 🌬 ☐Hot ☐Cold ☐Mild

Traveled from _____ to _____

Route Taken: _____

Start Mileage: _____ End Mileage: _____ Total Miles Traveled: _____

Sites Along The Way: _____

CAMPGROUND ☆☆☆☆☆

Campground Name: _____

Address: _____

Phone: _____ GPS: _____

Site #: _____ Ideal Site # (for next time): _____

Cost: _____ ☐ day ☐ week ☐ month

Memberships: _____

Altitude: _____ ☐ First Visit ☐ Return Visit

DRIVEWAY LENGTH: _____

☐easy access ☐back-in ☐antenna reception
☐loop ☐pull-through ☐satellite tv
☐paved ☐restrooms ☐cable tv
☐unpaved-graded ☐pet friendly ☐wifi:
☐picnic table ☐shade-partial/full   ☐free ☐$_____
☐fire ring ☐full sun cell phone carrier:
☐water ☐laundry
☐sewer ☐store/visitor center _____
☐electricity ☐pool/hot tub phone reception
☐15 amp ☐hiking trails ☆☆☆☆☆
☐30 amp ☐fishing water pressure
☐50 amp ☐firewood ☆☆☆☆☆

NOTES FOR NEXT TIME

(fees, check in/out times, discounts, directions, loud/quiet, etc)

NOTES

(Campground Pros/Cons, Traveling Companions, People Met, Places Visited, Things to Do, Restaurants, Journaling):

Made in the USA
Coppell, TX
04 October 2021

63441526R00059